12.75

LIVING
IN THE
GRASSLANDS

LIVING IN THE GRASSLANDS

CONSULTANTS TO THE
CULTURAL GEOGRAPHY SERIES:
MARC EICHEN
HILARY RENWICK

A CULTURAL GEOGRAPHY

LEO ROBERT

FRANKLIN WATTS 1988
NEW YORK LONDON TORONTO SYDNEY

Maps by Vantage Art, Inc.

Cover photographs by: (top left) © Carol Beckwith;
(top right) Kansas Department of Economic Development; (bottom left) Gene Ahrens/Shostal; (bottom
right) Shostal.

Photographs courtesy of: Sovfoto: pp. 20 (Tass), 22,
24, 27, 28, 30, 33 (Novosti), 34; Kenya Information
Services: pp. 40, 51; World Bank Photo: pp. 42 (James
Pickerell), 58 (Per Gunvall); Photo Researchers, Inc.:
pp. 43 (Ray Ellis), 45, 64, and 78 (Georg Gerster),
54 (Leonard Lee Rue III), 73 (Dave Repp), 74 (Van
Bucher); Carol Beckwith: pp. 46, 48, 50, 53, 57;
United Nations: p. 59 (Ian Steele); The Kansas State
Historical Society, Topeka: pp. 65, 67, 68, 69, 76.

Library of Congress Cataloging-in-Publication Data

Robert, Leo, 1948–
Living in the grasslands.

(A cultural geography)
Bibliography: p.
Includes index.
Summary: Compares and contrasts the cultural
geography of life in three different grassland
communities, in the Soviet Union, Kenya, and the
United States.
1. Anthropo-geography—Grasslands—Juvenile
literature. 2. Grasslands—Social life and customs—
Juvenile literature. 3. Grasslands—Description and
travel—Juvenile literature. [1. Anthropo-geography—
Grasslands. 2. Grasslands] I. Title. II. Series.
GF59.R63   1988   909'.0953   85-26601
ISBN 0-531-10146-0

CONTENTS

1

AN INTRODUCTION TO THE GRASSLANDS

THE WORLD'S GRASSLANDS

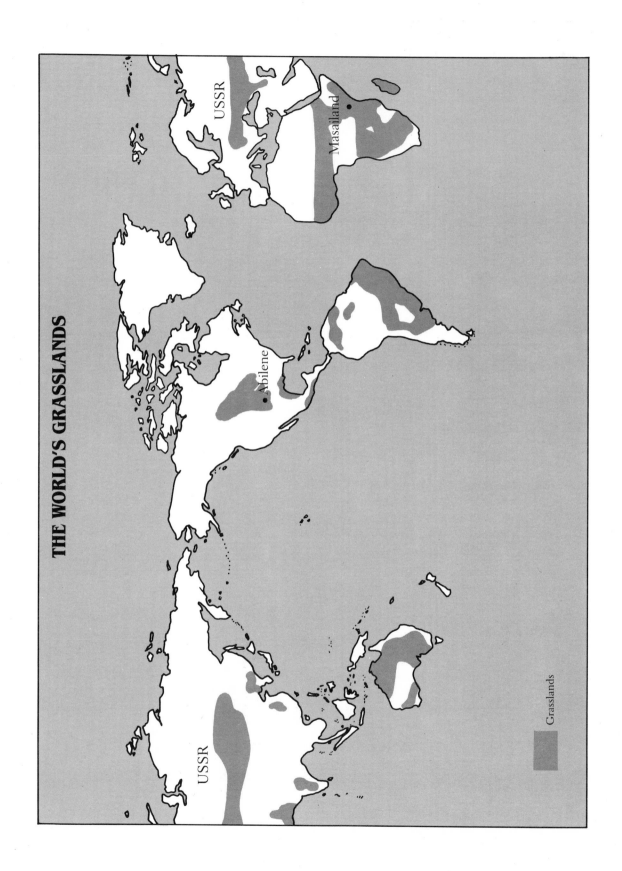

USSR

Masailand

Abilene

USSR

Grasslands

Picture yourself standing in a place where you can see almost from horizon to horizon. The land is generally flat and is planted with many different kinds of crops. Trees help break up the sameness of the meadows. From where you stand, you can see a town next to a river. Many of the buildings in the town are made of brick, while some are constructed of wood. Electric power lines run alongside the streets.

Close your eyes and the scene changes to a different, less familiar place. The land has a flat floor with some steep hills nearby. The big sky looms overhead. Instead of single farmhouses, you see a circle of dung-plastered houses. The ground is parched and dry. In the distance a small girl is carrying a bundle of twigs almost as big as she is. Cattle are corralled nearby.

Close your eyes once again and imagine another scene. The sky is the biggest part of your view, with gently rolling hills stretching on all sides. Even rows of wheat march into the distance. You are standing near a two-story white farmhouse, with big cottonwoods shading it and a small vegetable garden near the back door.

You have just been to a collective farm in the Soviet Union; Sowakla, a Masai village in Africa's Great Rift Valley; and Abilene, Kansas, in the United States. These three places are part of the world's mid-latitude *grassland* region.

All the world's grasslands have certains things in common. These include:

A *generally dry climate and sparse vegetation*—These semi-arid lands receive between 10 and 20 inches (25 and 50 cm) of rain each year. However, some areas may receive 30 or even 40 inches (76 to 101 cm) a year. With a hot summer and a mild winter, most of the rain comes from summer thunderstorms. The amount of rain is enough for grasses and shrubs to grow as natural vegetation. Some grassland areas may even receive enough rain to support a limited variety of trees.

Low population density—The world's grasslands have low human population densities. This means they have very few people in comparison with some other areas.

Transportation problems—Because there are so few people, travel between settlements is time-consuming and difficult.

An economy based on grain and cattle production—Crops that require a great deal of rain, such as corn, cannot survive in grassland areas without expensive irrigation. Growing wheat and raising cattle require less rain.

Drought as a natural hazard—Rainfall in the grasslands is not the same from year to year. There may be several wetter-than-average years in a row. Then several very dry years may follow. Human disaster can be the result, as cattle die and crops wither.

Dependence on world systems—Even if grassland settlements are remote and isolated, they are still tied to worldwide economic systems. For example, if a drought in the Soviet Union or Africa leads to a drop in wheat production in these areas, then American farmers may sell more wheat to them. Economic and climatic patterns tie grasslands and human beings together around the world. Only the most remote communities lack these global ties.

This book will compare and contrast the cultural geography of life in three different grassland communities. In addition to learning about the grassland communities, you will learn about the art and science of geography. You will also learn how cultural geographers study regions, and how they view the relationship between people and their natural environment.

WHAT IS CULTURAL GEOGRAPHY?

Cultural geographers study the interwoven lives of people and their environments. Cultural geographers ask such questions as: How did the people who live here get here? How did they decide where to settle and how to make a living? How have they influenced their environment (land and climate) and how has it affected them?

A major focus of cultural geography is how *culture* and *environment* fit together. By environment, we mean the physical features of the world around us: the air, water, plant life, soils, and rocks that make up the world's biosphere. The biosphere is the envelope of life surrounding the globe.

Culture is a way of life devised by human beings for getting along with the environment and each other. It is made up of beliefs, knowledge, religion, technology, economy, art, science, medicine, and philosophy. These are just a few of the elements of a culture. People around the world have put these elements together in different ways to create many diverse cultures.

HOW CULTURAL GEOGRAPHERS STUDY REGIONS

A *region* is an area within which elements of culture or environment are similar. Outside the region, the elements are different. For example, if farmers in a certain area all grow the same crop, then you can draw a line around that area on a map and call it a region. Actually, though, regions are more complicated. A region is usually made up of several elements that overlap unevenly. For example, look at Figure 2 on page 11. It is a map of the world, in which rainfall and vegetation patterns overlap. It separates the world into regions based on rainfall and vegetation.

Geographers can use information to map regions around the globe—on a world scale. Or they can look for more detailed regions at the scale of the nation. For example, the United States is separated into the Northeast, the Middle Atlantic, the Deep South, the Midwest, the Gulf States, the Southwest, and other regions, based on both objective and subjective information. Geographers gather objective information by observing and counting. This kind of information can include: rainfall, religion, settlement patterns, and vegetation. Geographers gather subjective information by carefully noting what people say and do in their daily lives or by listening to or reading the stories people tell one another.

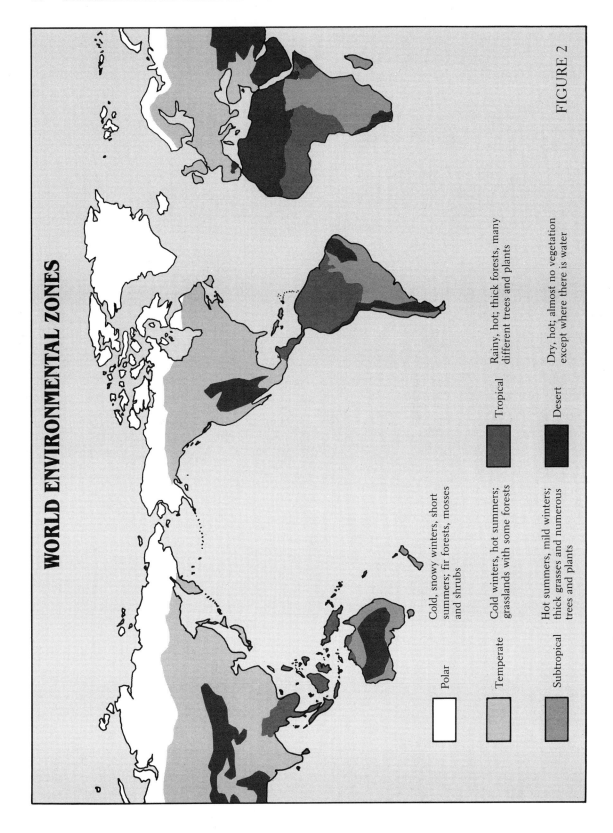

WORLD ENVIRONMENTAL ZONES

Polar — Cold, snowy winters, short summers; fir forests, mosses and shrubs

Temperate — Cold winters, hot summers; grasslands with some forests

Subtropical — Hot summers, mild winters; thick grasses and numerous trees and plants

Tropical — Rainy, hot; thick forests, many different trees and plants

Desert — Dry, hot; almost no vegetation except where there is water

FIGURE 2

Subjective information tells geographers what region people believe they live in and how these people think their region is different from surrounding places. For example, in the United States, a woman might say she is a Southerner because she has spent an important part of her life, her childhood, for example, in the South.

The three grassland communities described in this book are examples of *core areas*. These are areas where many objective and subjective elements of culture and environment overlap. As you move away from the core of a region, there will be fewer similar elements. As this happens, the region will gradually become more like the areas it borders. Often it is hard to decide what are the boundaries, or edges, of a region. For example, if you move east across Kansas, there is more rain and more corn. And there are fewer cattle ranches. As you move from the inland region of Kenya toward the coast, fewer families raise cattle and more raise cassava and yams. You are moving out of one region and into another. The boundaries between regions are not sharp, they are very gradual.

The more information used to define a region, the smaller the region is likely to be. For example, the world can be divided into big regions based on rainfall. But just imagine how many tiny regions you would have if, on top of rainfall, you laid down patterns of vegetation, religion, favorite sports, and favorite desserts! Cultural geographers must decide what information to use when defining a region. They must also decide how much of this information must overlap to include a place within a region.

Figure 3 is a *model*. A model is a simplification of the real thing. In this case it is a simplification of a region. Figure 3 shows how objective and subjective information overlap to form a region, and how the core area gets smaller as more measures are added.

HOW ENVIRONMENT AND CULTURE FIT TOGETHER

You may be asking yourself how environment and culture fit together in the world's grassland region. First, the environment does not determine the type of culture in a region. That is, rainfall, vegetation, and sunshine do not completely dictate how human beings live. If people were only controlled by their environment, then all people in all grasslands around the world would be leading the same lives. But this is not so. Human choices and decision-making are not solely at the mercy of the environment. However, neither does culture entirely control the environment. If people completely controlled the grasslands, then all people in all the grasslands around the world might be leading very different lives. But this is not so, because we have seen that there are many similarities among grassland communities in the ways that the land is used.

Culture and environment interact. That is, each influences the other. For example, in Kansas the environment does not provide enough rainfall to grow soybeans. This means that the environment influences culture by limiting what can be grown. But, then, farmers may use irrigation to provide the necessary extra mois-

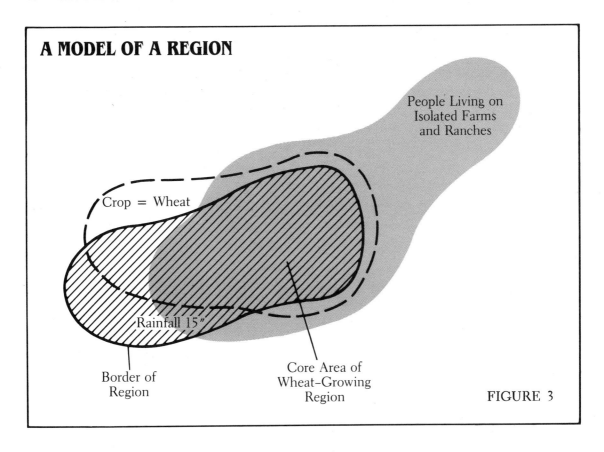

A MODEL OF A REGION

People Living on
Isolated Farms
and Ranches

Crop = Wheat

Rainfall 15″

Border of
Region

Core Area of
Wheat–Growing
Region

FIGURE 3

ture for growing soybeans. If enough farmers use irrigation, they may use so much water that there will not be enough for other needs. Then water would become more costly in the future, since it would have to come from deeper wells or from farther away. In this case, human culture can influence the environment by determining how much water will be available in the long run. It may appear that culture has conquered the environment. But natural hazards such as drought can quickly overcome many improvements and changes. During the 1930s, several dry years created desert-like conditions in areas of the American Middle

West. Thousands of farms were wiped out. In earlier, better times, people thought they had conquered nature.

Some cultural geographers believe that the more a culture uses its natural resources, the greater the risk of natural disaster. For example, wheat and cattle production in the world's grasslands allow agriculture to prosper in years of plentiful rain. During these good years, people have enough food and money. Often, farmers will plant more fields with wheat and buy more cattle, as there is plenty of water and grass to support them. When rain does not come, however, people who rely on this way of making a living suffer greatly. The planted wheat shrivels in the sun, and the cattle die of starvation and thirst.

When studying the world's grassland region, cultural geographers may ask the following questions:

■ How have culture and the environment interacted in this region?

■ How do people as children learn to use their environment?

■ If culture or the environment changes, will these people be able to keep up with the changes?

■ How many families can the environment support?

■ If the culture changes, can the environment support more or fewer families?

■ How do people protect themselves from natural hazards such as drought?

■ How successful or costly are their hazard-protection methods?

As you study the world's mid-latitude grasslands, you can ask similar questions. These questions can also help you learn more about the region in which you live.

2

VIRIATINO

A SOVIET GRASSLANDS VILLAGE

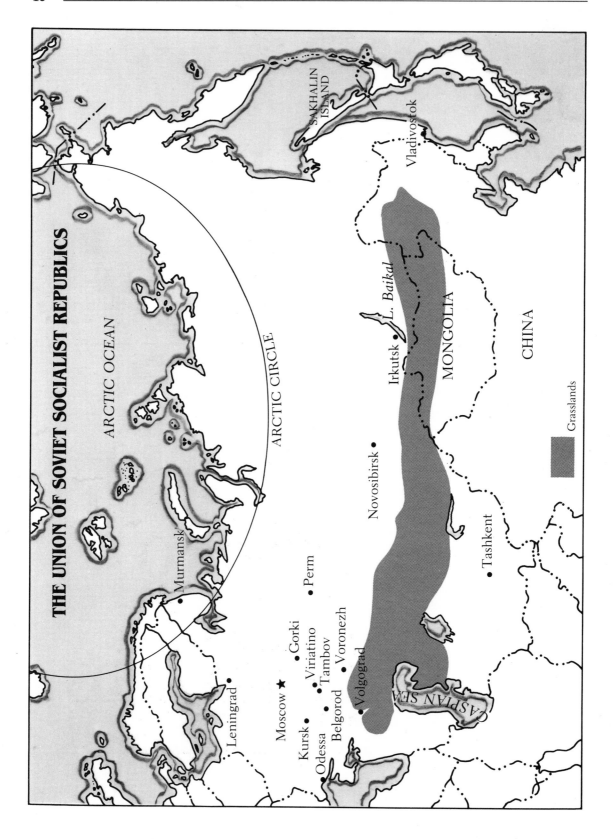

THE UNION OF SOVIET SOCIALIST REPUBLICS

ARCTIC OCEAN

ARCTIC CIRCLE

Murmansk

Leningrad

Moscow ★

Gorki

Perm

Kursk
Odessa
Belgorod
Voronezh
Tambov
Viriatino
Volgograd

CASPIAN SEA

Novosibirsk

Tashkent

Irkutsk
L. Baikal

MONGOLIA

CHINA

SAKHALIN ISLAND

Vladivostok

Grasslands

It's early fall in Viriatino, a tiny village in the grasslands of the Soviet Union. Anna Kulikov rises at dawn to prepare the day's food for her husband, Oleg, and her two children, Ivan and Natasha. She cooks on a Russian stove. This combination range and oven is no different from the one her grandmother used fifty years ago. The Russian stove is well suited to the area, a mixture of grasslands and forests. The grassy farmlands provide grains to be made into bread and the other foods that the people eat most often. The forests provide wood to be burned in the stove to cook the food and heat the houses.

After breakfast Oleg Kulikov goes to work on the nearby "Lenin's Way" *kolkhoz*, named after the early Soviet leader. This kolkhoz, or large collective farm, was created in 1930 when the Soviet government took control of the smaller farms of Viriatino and merged them into one. The government did this to many other farms throughout the Soviet Union in order to make the country's farming more productive. Today just about everyone in the village of more than 1,000 people belongs to the collective.

Oleg, like many of the other villagers, works in the collective farm fields cultivating crops. Anna does the household chores and takes care of the family's vegetable garden and livestock. The children go to school, where they get job training, like carpentry, and take courses, like physics. Ivan belongs to a hobby group for playing chess, a popular game in the Soviet Union. Natasha belongs to a group for singing and dancing.

In the evening the family gathers for supper. At the table they discuss a Tchaikovsky opera, *Evgeni Onegin*, that they listened to on the radio the night before. Young Ivan reports on the latest success of his volleyball team. A few months earlier, in the summer, they had no time to eat and talk together. The family was busy all day working on the collective farm.

THE GRASSLANDS ENVIRONMENT

Life in Viriatino centers on farming. The village lies within the *forest-steppe*, a narrow band of trees and grasslands that runs across the European part of the Soviet Union. The grassy steppe zone to the south has mostly *chernozem*, or black-earth soils. This kind of soil is among the most fertile in the world. The steppe also has a warm but dry climate. The forest zone to the north is generally wetter but has cooler air and less fertile soils. The forest-steppe region in between has the Soviet Union's best combination of soils, rainfall, and temperatures for growing grain crops and the trees that help to protect them. Farming is what most of the village people do for most of the year.

Temperatures in the grasslands are cool to moderate, ranging between an average of about 14° F (—10° C) in January and 68° F (20° C) in July. Yearly precipitation averages about 20 inches (50 cm), most of it coming between April and October. Snow stays on the ground for most of the winter.

Viriatino is surrounded by the Tambov Plain. This is a low, mostly flat region of many streams within the larger Oka-Don river lowlands of the Soviet Union's East European Plain. The elevation is only about 500 feet (152 m) above sea level. Most of the plain is tilled for crops: wheat, rice, sugar beets, sunflowers, and potatoes. Trees native to the area include oak, ash, maple, and linden. Much of the natural forest, however, has been destroyed by cutting. Orchards, consisting mainly of apple trees, have increased in importance to the economy in recent years, and Viriatino farmers take pride in growing them. The apples are used on the collective farm and sold in the cities.

The Tambov Plain lies within the Tambov Oblast. An *oblast* is a small political division of the Soviet Union. The Tambov Oblast is named after the city of Tambov, which, with about 280,000 people, is its largest city. Tambov, Belgorod, Voronezh, Kursk, and Lipetsk oblasts make up the Central Chernozem, or Black Earth, Region. This region covers an area of 65,000 square miles (168,000 sq km) with a population of about 8 million. One of the smaller regions of the Soviet Union, Central Chernozem is also one of the more important regions because of the potential its farming has for the national economy.

THE VILLAGE

Viriatino is in the Sosnov area of the Tambov Oblast, about 20 miles (32 km) north of Tambov. Several other small villages are nearby. Moscow, the capital city of the Soviet Union, lies about 200 miles (321 km) to the northwest in a forest zone. Volgograd, a major port city, lies about the same distance to the southeast in the steppe zone.

The area around Viriatino is primarily flat meadowland with some small hills and waterless stream valleys. Part of the area is forest. The village sits on higher ground where the Chelnovaya River meets the smaller Pishlyaika River. The flat areas on all sides of the village flood every spring when rain and melting snow swell the area streams.

Viriatino has one long main street running next to the Pishlyaika River. Two rows of houses stand on either side of this street. In addition, there are a few smaller side streets. A square in the main street marks the center of village social life. The village church, built in the square more than one hundred years ago, was closed by the government in 1933. The kolkhoz replaced it with a village club, where activities such as plays, movies, and lectures are held.

HISTORY OF AGRICULTURE AND LAND OWNERSHIP

Viriatino always had farmland, but not enough good farmland for everyone. Some plots have the rich chernozem soils, but many have less fertile ashy or sandy soils. The kolkhoz owns the better land in the area, while the villagers have small plots of poorer land for their private use. A constant struggle for ownership of the better land has been going on in the area since it was settled more than three hundred years ago.

The Soviet Union was known then as Russia. Many battles were fought between the Russians and the Tatars, who wanted to control the land. Tatars were Turkic peoples from the south who invaded Russia in the 1200s. The Tatars had already taken control of the steppe region. Soldiers known as *Cossacks* helped the Russians defeat the Tatars. These adventurous Russian fighters rode together in bands to battle the invaders and bring order to the area. Although many Cossacks were outlaws, they were given special privileges in return for their efforts. One privilege was ownership of large pieces of good land. For many years, poor Viriatino peasants had to farm the land for these Cossacks and other rich owners. As payment for their work, they received small plots of farmland of their own.

Because farming conditions were so good, the region developed into one of the country's most productive farming areas. This attracted many farming people into the area—many more than are usually found in rural areas. As late as the 1870s, provinces including Tambov were known as the breadbasket of Russia because they produced so much food. Later, railroads came to the area, making Viriatino and surrounding villages even more important as a food source for Moscow, the present-day Russian capital.

But the way that land was owned led to poor farming methods. Government reforms, beginning in 1861, tried but failed to transfer land ownership from the rich to the poor. To insure that everyone received at least some of the scarce rich farmland, land was given out in small, narrow strips. As a result, peasants often owned several small pieces of land that were far apart. They had to use a three-field system of cultivation, in which they divided their land into winter, spring, and fallow, or unplanted fields. In this way they could plant different crops in different fields so that the fields would not soon lose their nutrients. But farming scattered strips was more difficult than farming one large plot. It also required more workers.

Because there were too many people in the Viriatino area for all to earn a good living from the land, many remained poor. They could afford to use only crude wooden plows to till the soil, and those did not dig deep enough for proper planting. Peasants often did not bother to fertilize the soil. Much of the land was eroded. Many fields became overgrown with weeds. Productivity decreased each year. By the 1880s, the steppe provinces to the south, where land holdings were larger and farming methods more advanced, became the country's new breadbasket.

When the first farm machines— horse-drawn threshers and reapers—were developed around 1900, only the rich landowners and *kulaks*, or rich peasants, could afford them. Besides, most peasant plots of land were too small to use these machines.

Land reforms of 1906 tried to break up the three-field system and take away larger pieces from rich owners. This attempt at reform failed. Conditions grew worse for the peasants after the start of World War I in 1914. Most of the men

*A village in Russia before
the revolution*

were drafted into the army, thus depriving the farmland of its main workers.

In 1917, a bloody revolution took place in Russia. The revolution overthrew the *tsar* who had ruled the country with absolute power. With the overthrow of the tsar, an entire way of life came to an end.

Russia's new leaders promised "Land, Peace, and Bread." The peasants thought the land would become theirs. But it didn't. The communist government of the Soviet Union (the new name for Russia) kept the three-field system. Crop failures resulted in famine during the middle 1920s, but conditions improved by the late 1920s.

Then the government decided to collectivize the land. Large farms would be formed by putting together many smaller ones. The farms would be worked by the peasants, but owned by the Soviet government. Many peasants were against the idea of taking care of the government-owned farms, but they had little choice. The "Lenin's Way" collective farm of Viriatino, started in 1930, became one of the largest farms in the region.

LABOR AND OCCUPATIONS

The villagers of Viriatino have always been farming people. But when other industries developed in the Tambov area in the late 1800s and early 1900s, many peasant farmers worked in them. Usually they continued to farm and tried to earn more money from these new jobs during the seasons when they were not farming. But the peasants generally did not earn much money, because the landowners and kulaks controlled the new industries just as they controlled the land.

From the large forest next to Viriatino, trees were cut down for logs, building planks, and fuel. Kulaks controlled this business, and few of the poorer peasants made money from it. Cattle, horses, and sheep were transported from the steppes near the Caspian Sea about 600 miles (965 km) to the southwest. This led to the trading of meat in the Viriatino area, but only the kulaks had enough money to participate. Peasants carted grain and other farm products from the larger farms to city markets, but the railroads arrived during the late 1800s and took over this trade. Some peasants made the fired bricks needed for building, but the only clay suitable for making bricks was found on the rich landowners' property. Peasant women bleached linen for clothing next to the rivers, where the grassy banks made a convenient surface. But this business slowed as manufactured cloth became available in the cities in the early 1900s. As a result, the Russian tradition of home-spinning and weaving came to a stop. A few peasants were sheet-metal workers, housepainters, and tailors, but there was not enough work to keep them busy in these occupations.

Peasants looked for work in other provinces. Many tried coal-mining in the Donbass region to the south, but the work was hard, unhealthy, and low-paying. Also, mining lasted only six months of the year, stopping during spring when rising underground waters flooded the mines. Peasants stopped looking for other work by the late

*Hungry peasants during
the time of the tsars*

1920s, when farming was beginning to become productive again.

ENVIRONMENTAL PROBLEMS

When Viriatino prospered as a farming village during the middle 1800s, the people thought of the land and its resources as limitless. Trees could be cut down and water could be used without care, because there would always be plenty of both. The soil could be planted and replanted without care. The people loved the land, but they thought the land could take care of itself.

During the late 1800s the peasants began to have other ideas about the land. Soil erosion became widespread due to poor farming methods. Poor plowing methods, in particular, destroyed the soil's protective cover. Wide-scale lumbering around 1900 increased erosion, and no new trees were planted as replacements. Without proper crop rotation or fertilization, soils were stripped of rich minerals. Frequent fires, flooding, and dry spells made farming and living even more difficult.

SETTLEMENT AND HOUSES

Viriatino started out small and grew slowly. Unlike the steppe villagers to the south, who built their houses in valleys for protection from cold winds, the first Viriatino settlers cleared away woods to build on the higher land. They did this to escape the flooding of the rivers in spring. As more houses were built, they formed a single row. They faced south to get the full warmth of the sun and to leave space in the back for gardens and meadows by the river. Farm buildings were built on the other side of the street.

By the 1870s, as Viriatino became more crowded, new streets were built. Small lots were laid out to fit in as many houses as possible. A second row of houses was squeezed in on the main street by narrowing the strip of land next to the road and moving storage places out of town. Later, as families continued to break up and the demand for houses grew, they had to be built at the edge of the village. In the late 1800s and early 1900s, Viriatino's business center began to develop around the church.

In recent years more storage sheds have been moved out of the village to make room for wider streets as well as new trees and shrubs. Most newer houses in the village now have enough space between them to keep fire from spreading. Many streets in Viriatino still have only one row of houses extending for long distances.

About half of the houses in Viriatino were built before 1917. Most homes in the early 1800s were crude, one-room log huts. Not much attention was paid to how houses looked, because the peasants had little money for fixing them and fires often burned them to the ground. After the peasant reforms of 1861, when the large families started to break up into smaller family units, more houses were needed. When more peasants got income from working in other regions, and carpentry improved, larger wooden and brick houses

Farming methods used in the 1800s

could be built. A brick house was a status symbol, showing others how much money the family had. Brick also stood up against fire, although most brick houses had thatched roofs made of straw. When tin became available around 1900, some people changed to tin roofs for better fire protection. But most peasants could afford neither brick houses nor tin roofs.

FAMILY LIFE

Before 1917, Viriatino households were made up mostly of large families of several generations living together. The rights and duties of family members were laid out with strict guidelines. The oldest man headed the family, and the oldest son directed the family farm. The wife of the head of the family was in charge of household duties. Young girls helped with housework, such as spinning and weaving. Women and children did garden work. Activities were done at the same time every day.

In those days, keeping a large family together was the best way to farm the land. Because the family had several small plots in separate areas, large numbers of workers were needed. Peasant families who could afford to own horses, oxen, or cows needed extra members to work them. The few poor families who had more farmhands than their farms needed could get extra income by sending family members out to other regions to work in industry.

Large families staying together became less typical during the 1880s. Other industries came to Viriatino that required fewer workers. But most families had to stay together to keep their farms going.

WHAT THE PEOPLE ATE

The peasants of Viriatino ate mostly bread and grain products, because that is what the farmers grew. They used mainly rye flour, because they couldn't grow wheat and it had to be bought at the market. Peasant women baked rye bread once a week in the Russian stove. Pancakes and blintzes were often made from rye flour. *Kvass*, a fermented beverage made from dried black bread and sometimes prepared with vegetables, was an important part of the diet. The main hot dish, served almost every day, was cabbage soup, later known as borscht. Another popular soup was made from wheat flour and cooked with potatoes or lard. Peasants also enjoyed kasha, the potato pulp left from cooking this soup, with milk or oil. The poorer peasants ate far less meat and eggs than those who were better off. Few people owned livestock, and many had to sell their eggs for extra money.

TRADITION, RELIGION, CULTURE

Viriatino was a village of strong traditions before collectivization. Although Tambov and the surrounding provinces were within a few hundred miles of Moscow, the villages of the region remained isolated. There were few roads, and those that did exist were in poor condition. The people of Viriatino had little reason to travel other than to look for work in other regions. Thus, they had almost no knowledge of city life. What little news they got reached them by word of mouth. Few villagers could read, so the absence of newspapers didn't matter. Many peasant children never went to school. Before 1890, Viriatino had no cultural organizations, like libraries or clubs. Most of the village customs were determined by the church.

Everyone belonged to the church. The people of Viriatino met their daily problems with strong religious beliefs. All aspects of family life, including work days, use of free time, and diet, were determined by the dates of the church calendar. Rituals were performed throughout the year, most of them related to farming. Religious holidays, like Christmas and Easter, were the most important times of the year.

THE IMPACT OF COLLECTIVIZATION

The collectivization that began after the Communist Revolution of 1917 brought great changes to Viriatino. The breakup of large families into smaller ones continued as families needed fewer members to work on the kolkhoz. Increased farm production on the kolkhoz boosted the Viriatino economy. This changed the way the people used what they had. Today they have more money to spend on a greater variety of foods and city-made products.

Health has improved greatly. In the past, unsanitary conditions contributed to a high rate of disease and early death. Now the people are more concerned about keeping their surroundings clean. Steambaths are very popular, and there are more than eighty of them in Viriatino. Insects were

a major health problem. The use of pesticides had rid the village of insects.

Improvements in the standard of living have resulted in bigger and better houses. Since 1957 Viriatino builders have been using bricks made on the collective to put up new houses for the farmers. Houses now have electricity, which became available in the late 1940s. Many houses have plastered walls on the inside, and more wooden houses are shingled and painted. The people pay more attention to improving the insides of their houses too. They buy the latest furniture and household items made in the cities. Almost all houses have front gardens planted with flowers and trees. These add beauty to the street and protect houses from wind and dust.

For many collective farmers, the house consists of one room, made up of a kitchen and living area. In recent years some people have begun to separate the kitchen or add one to the existing building. Also, there has been a trend toward multi-room houses, including kitchen, dining room, living room, and bedroom.

Many changes in Viriatino have been made by the kolkhoz. Several newer buildings have been built in the village center to house administrative and cultural activities. Other kolkhoz structures in and around Viriatino include industrial workshops, known as "garages," repair shops, warehouses, and a hydroelectric station and water tower. Several large brick barns have been built to store kolkhoz grain and dairy products and to house livestock.

When the church was closed after the revolution, the people were encouraged to give up their religion. After a while

A collective farm. The private
homes and gardens of the
farmers are visible.

A new street on a state farm

they did, especially the young. Some of the church customs are still observed, but mostly by the older people out of habit. Religious beliefs gave way to Communist teachings: respect for public property, working on the collective farm, and using education to better their lives.

With collectivization Viriatino workers have fit into three groups. The main group, more than half of the families, works on the collective farm, in fields or with livestock. Two smaller groups are the families of the collective's managers and the specialized workers and families who do work outside of the farm.

"Lenin's Way" farm workers are divided into *brigades,* or groups of about one hundred people each. Each brigade does one kind of work on a plot of kolkhoz land permanently assigned to it. Most brigades cultivate field crops, the major work of the kolkhoz. Crop cultivation is seasonal, however, leaving workers some time to care for their own smaller plots later in the fall. Cattle breeding has become popular on the Viriatino collective because the people can make more money from this than from field work. People make some money from selling their own produce and livestock, but not nearly as much as they can make working on the kolkhoz. As in the past, larger families generally make more money. Their income is determined by the total days in the year that family members work on the farm.

The collective farm needs many specialized workers who know about the latest farming methods, stock breeding, and machinery. Before 1958, a Machine and Tractor Station supplied the kolkhoz with farm equipment and workers who did specialized jobs. Since then, the kolkhoz has taken over jobs requiring special skills. Training programs are now offered for workers to specialize, and brigade leaders attend weekly courses to increase their knowledge of farming.

A few Viriatino people work outside the collective farm. Some work in factories or plants in nearby cities. But most of the people in nonfarming trades or professions are part of the kolkhoz.

LIFE ON THE COLLECTIVE FARM TODAY

Today the modern collective farm family is a small unit. It usually has three to six members, consisting of parents and their children, not unlike the Kulikov family. Young couples leave home soon after marriage to settle in another house, often next to the house of their parents. Some leave the collective to look for factory work in the cities. Young people who cannot afford their own house create separate living space for themselves within their parents' houses.

All adults within a family have equal rights. The oldest man no longer runs the family. A married son may be responsible for handling family matters, but women usually share in deciding how the family's money will be spent. The people have a saying: "everything for the children." Much of the family money is spent on goods for the children. Oleg and Anna Kulikov also give their children much more

*The harvesting of wheat on
a collective farm*

freedom than parents did in the past. Young Ivan and Natasha even have a voice in making family decisions.

MODERN GOVERNMENT

All social life in Viriatino is controlled by the village *soviet*, its governing council. The soviet determines procedures for elections, which are important events in village life. Several meetings are held to choose candidates who want to be elected to positions within the village soviet, in collective farm management, or to state-wide offices. After the candidates campaign, reporting to the people what they have achieved in office, voting takes place in the high school. Election day is a holiday, a festive occasion. The one who is elected chairperson of the collective farm must then make regular reports to the village soviet on how work is going on the farm. The collective farm management and village soviet meet often to discuss and handle economic and cultural problems.

The village soviet also determines taxes, settles disputes among the people, and supervises cultural and educational activities. The soviet takes particular responsibility for educating the people in Communist politics.

THE COLLECTIVE FARM ECONOMY

The collective farm controls the Viriatino economy. It does this by controlling the land. About four-fifths of the collective farm land is used for planting crops. The remaining one-fifth is divided between meadowland and forest. The kolkhoz management board, elected by the collective farmers, plans all work and production. But the central government of the Soviet Union makes all major decisions for the nation's collective farms. The central government in Moscow decides things like how much wheat should be produced and how many days workers must work each year.

Every year most of the farmland around Viriatino is planted with cereal grains and bean-pod. Rye is still the main crop, but oats and millet are planted as well. Smaller amounts of land are planted with potatoes and vegetables, fodder crops for livestock, *mahorka* (a variety of tobacco), hemp, flax, and sunflowers.

Livestock raising and dairy farming are second to field crops in importance to the kolkhoz economy. Some areas of meadowland have small hills that are covered with bushes, making them difficult to mow. But livestock can graze in these areas.

Bricks are made from the clay soil on the kolkhoz, and peat is available for fuel. The farmers, who otherwise find it difficult to get fuel as the supply of trees dwindles, may keep half of whatever fuel supplies they gather. The other half goes to the kolkhoz.

LOCAL DIET

The people of Viriatino still eat bread and grain products, but most of the traditional dishes are no longer eaten. Today farm families of the Viriatino collective have their own small plot of land to farm. Almost every family owns cows, pigs, sheep, and poultry. Because they get most of their income from working on the collective farm, the farmers can better afford to eat what they grow. Meat, eggs, vegetables, and sweets have become a bigger part of the diet. Wheat bread is popular because the kolkhoz has succeeded in growing wheat where small farms failed in the past.

Various foods are eaten according to the season. Winter foods are mostly grain dishes, potatoes, pickled cucumbers, sauerkraut, pork, fresh ham, beef, and vegetable oils used for cooking. Closer to spring, veal, rendered lard, and butter are eaten. Summer foods include milk products, fresh vegetables, and fresh fish. Most houses now have attic space for storing vegetables and fruits and for drying grain.

In many Viriatino houses cooking is still done on the Russian stove, which is made of bricks covered with clay. In the front is a wood-burning range for cooking. In the back is a high bread oven. The Russian stove forms a broad stairway on top, with steps that are used for beds for children and older people.

VIRIATINO WORLD VIEW TODAY

A big gap still remains between the country villages and the cities in the Soviet Union. But the people of present-day Viriatino are more aware of the outside world. Traffic to and from the village has increased. Tambov Province has more than 7,000 miles (11,265 km) of roads, though only a few are paved, and more than 500 miles (805 km) of railroads. More young people are leaving the village for jobs and life in the cities. But they maintain close contact with the villagers. They often come back to visit and share their experiences and new ideas.

Listening to the radio and watching television have become popular in Viriatino. At least half of the families subscribe to newspapers, especially the national newspapers, *Pravda* and *Izvestia*. But the people also read local newspapers, magazines, and a farming publication, *Selskoe Kosiastvo*. All but a few people can read, and most families often use the village library. One of the major goals of the Soviet government has been to educate the people by encouraging them to read.

The people enjoy cultural events, especially concerts of folk songs, movies, and productions at the local club. They often attend lectures on topics like farming and childbearing. The young people are active in sports, like skiing, track, volleyball, and football (called soccer in the United States). The cultural life of Viriatino, like farming, is seasonal. In winter, events are well organized because the people have the time to meet. In summer, everybody is too busy working in the fields to spend much time on other activities.

The teachers of Viriatino and the better educated citizens, known as *intelligentsia*, influence how the people speak, act, and dress. The people respect them and follow their example.

MODERN USE OF THE ENVIRONMENT

The people of Viriatino are more careful in how they use the environment, but the problems of the past have not gone away.

A farm family taking a break. The
samovar in the center of the table
is used to boil water for tea.

*Irrigated pastures on
a collective farm*

Drought and soil erosion are the two biggest problems. Because the soil is fine grained and blows away easily, wind erosion is significant during dry periods. Wind erosion is aided by the wide-scale plowing of grasses and cutting of trees, both of which rob the soil of protective cover.

These activities and the ruts left by farm vehicles are responsible for soil erosion. Deep gullies form in the unprotected soil, and streams form in them, primarily during the frequent periods of flooding. This washes the soil away.

Throughout the forest-steppe region, the Soviet government has fought back by planting *shelterbelts*. These are barriers of trees and shrubs that protect crops from the wind and storms. In other places, *reforestation*—the planting of numerous young trees or seeds to replace trees that were cut down—is being carried out to fight soil erosion.

The "Lenin's Way" collective farm has planted many trees to protect Viriatino's land against erosion. But it has made many more improvements in farming methods. Unlike the Viriatino peasants of the past, kolkhoz workers apply mineral fertilizers to the soil on a regular basis. Carefully planned crop rotation, controlled grazing of pasture lands, and modern farming methods like contour plowing have helped to restore the farmland. Use of irrigation systems to water the fields and modern machinery, including tractors, combines, and trucks, has greatly increased the land's productivity.

Another problem of the past—too many farm workers in the area for the limited amount of farmland—is also being solved. A great variety of small industries is developing in the area's bigger towns and cities. Tambov, for example, is known for the manufacture of railway equipment, electric motors, automobile parts, and chemical products. Michurinsk, to the west, is famous for plant-breeding experiments. Village farmers are finding jobs in these places and moving there. As a result, fewer farm people are making demands on the limited farmlands of Viriatino.

HOW THE PEOPLE VIEW THE LAND

The Communist revolution of 1917 gave Russian farmers collective ownership of the land, but it took away all hope of having their own land. "Village" writers like Fyodor Abramov have sharply criticized the changes that collectivization brought to the small Russian villages. The writers see collective ownership as a system that has weakened the people's closeness with the land. They see farming people who have less pride in their work, and in themselves, because the land belongs to everyone now. Finally, they blame more recent farming failures on the changes in the villages. On the other hand, members of the Soviet intelligentsia argue that collective farming on the kolkhoz has not hurt the villagers, but has *saved* them from the many farming failures of the past.

The people of Viriatino are slow to change, but they have changed. They once dreamed of individually owning the land of grasses and trees themselves. Now they must be content to own it together.

3

SOWAKLA

A VILLAGE
IN AFRICA'S
GRASSLANDS

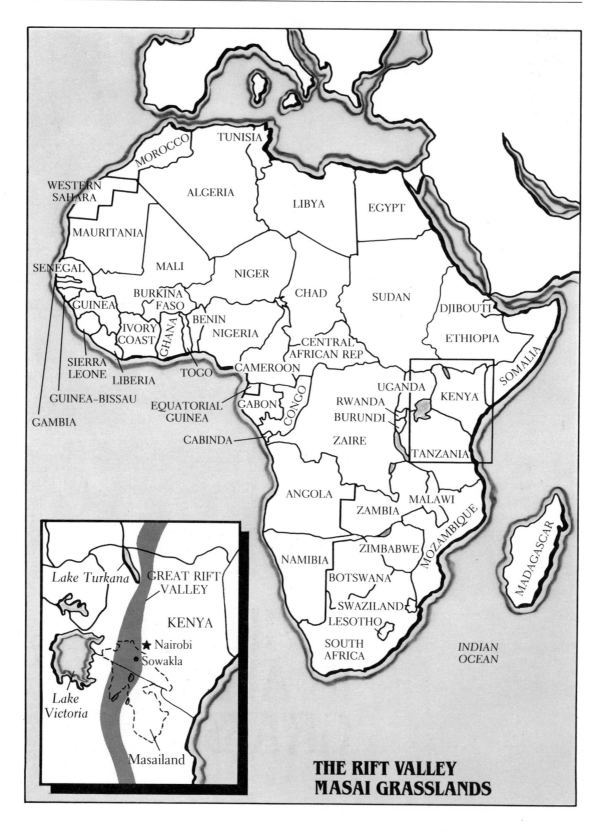

THE RIFT VALLEY
MASAI GRASSLANDS

MOROCCO
TUNISIA
WESTERN
SAHARA
ALGERIA
LIBYA
EGYPT
MAURITANIA
SENEGAL
MALI
NIGER
GUINEA
BURKINA
FASO
CHAD
SUDAN
DJIBOUTI
BENIN
IVORY
COAST
GHANA
NIGERIA
ETHIOPIA
SIERRA
LEONE
LIBERIA
TOGO
CAMEROON
CENTRAL
AFRICAN REP
SOMALIA
GUINEA-BISSAU
EQUATORIAL
GUINEA
GABON
CONGO
UGANDA
RWANDA
BURUNDI
KENYA
GAMBIA
CABINDA
ZAIRE
TANZANIA
ANGOLA
MALAWI
ZAMBIA
MOZAMBIQUE
MADAGASCAR
ZIMBABWE
NAMIBIA
BOTSWANA
SWAZILAND
LESOTHO
SOUTH
AFRICA
INDIAN
OCEAN

Lake Turkana
GREAT RIFT
VALLEY
KENYA
★ Nairobi
● Sowakla
Lake
Victoria
Masailand

The dark-skinned boy standing beside the thorn bush is tending his family's goats. The spear he holds in one hand is for fighting off any swift cheetah that might attack the animals. The umbrella in his other hand is for protecting himself against one of the rainy cloudbursts that are frequent during this wet season. The twelve-year-old boy does not go to school, because his people rely on him to watch over the animals all day. Besides, he is getting ready to become a *moran*, or warrior. He will be responsible for hunting lions and protecting his tribe.

The tribe is the Pastoral Masai, one of a large group of Masai tribes who live in eastern Africa. The Pastoral Masai number about 115,000 and live in grassland villages, mostly along the Great Rift Valley in Kenya. While many Masai tribes practice farming, the Pastoral Masai live entirely from herding the cattle and other animals they own. Because there is not always enough water for their cattle to drink, or grass for them to eat, the Pastoral Masai sometimes must take the cattle from their villages for several months to look for more water and grass.

At night the boy urges his family's goats back to the Sowakla village compound. Like most Pastoral Masai villages, it consists of crude houses designed for living in only part of the year. The boy lives in one with his parents, brothers and sisters, and baby animals. When he becomes a warrior at age fifteen, he will have his own house in a separate area. The houses

here form a circle inside a high fence. The Masai keep their animals well-protected at night in the opening in the middle of the village.

THE RIFT VALLEY MASAI GRASSLANDS

The Ngong Hills drop sharply from Kenya's eastern highlands, about 20 miles (32 km) west of the capital city of Nairobi. At their base lie several Pastoral Masai villages scattered across the sometimes grassy Rift Valley floor. The Rift Valley is a deep valley, up to a half-mile deep in some places, that runs north-to-south through much of the eastern half of Africa. Generally 20 to 35 miles (32 to 56 km) wide, the valley is 200 miles (322 km) wide in northern Kenya. The Rift Valley was probably formed by a variety of forces, including volcanic action. The flat valley floor has many volcanic plugs, cones, and lake beds.

Sowakla and other Pastoral Masai villages on the Rift Valley floor west of Nairobi lie in the Rift Valley Masai Grasslands. This specific grassland region is actually just a small part of the much larger *Acacia-Thermeda* community of open grasslands with scattered trees. This type of grasslands is also called *savanna*. This zone extends about 200 miles (322 km) east-to-west on the southern side of Kenya's Mau Hills. Vegetation in the Rift Valley Masai Grasslands part consists of acacia trees and shrubs and such grasses

A view of a major street in
Nairobi, the capital of Kenya.

as star grass and red oat grass. Wild animals include the rhinoceros, gerenuk, wildebeest, zebra, oryx, and giraffe. All are found in small numbers, because most are now confined to game reserves. This grassland area is suitable for the grazing of domestic animals, like cows and goats, but not very good for farming.

At about 1° south latitude, the Rift Valley Masai Grasslands are not far from the equator. Even on the deep floor of the Rift Valley, the Masai villages are at a relatively high elevation, ranging between 4,000 and 6,500 feet (1,220 and 1,980 m) above sea level. Despite the high elevation, the equatorial climate is hot for most of the year. This climate is classified as *tropical continental* or *tropical savanna*, and its high temperatures vary greatly with differences in elevation. Precipitation is limited, averaging between 20 and 30 inches (50 and 75 cm) a year. Most of it falls in the months between November and May. During this rainy season the lakes fill, the many streams overflow, and the land gradually turns green. During the dry season that follows, the lakes and streams dry up under the hot sun. The land turns gray and dusty, and the grasses and many animals die. The Pastoral Masai herd their cattle near permanent waters in the dry season. In the wet season they move to temporary waters formed by the rains, leaving the dry-season pastures to reestablish themselves.

Most of the soil in the Rift Valley Masai Grasslands is tropical black-earth soil. This soil does not drain water very well. This results in much evaporation and is responsible for the general lack of trees in wide areas of open grasslands.

Masai peoples live in a large, but shrinking area of south-central Kenya known as Masailand. Masailand has twelve sections, their sizes determined by how many Masai live in them. Much of the Rift Valley Masai Grasslands west of Nairobi lie in *Keekonyokie*, one of the smaller sections. The closeness to Kenya's capital city brings the Pastoral Masai in villages like Sowakla closer to the outside world than many other Masai. But the Pastoral Masai themselves have changed very little over several thousand years.

HISTORY OF THE PASTORAL MASAI

The Pastoral Masai honor cattle, and almost everything they have comes from the cattle they own. This is because they believe that their god, *Engai*, ordered them to be cattle-herders. In his book, *Maasai*, Tepelit Ole Saitoti, a Masai warrior who is now a conservationist in Kenya, repeats a legend he heard often as a youngster:

"Engai had three children to whom he gave three gifts. The first received an arrow to make his living by hunting, the second a hoe to dig the land and grow crops, and the third a stick to use in herding cattle. This third son, whose name was Natero Kop, was the father of the Maasai, who have since that time been the proud keepers of cattle. So, in the shadow of Mount Lengai, the Maasai have decided to observe the many sunrises and fiery sunsets and to guard their cattle grazing on the golden savannah. Standing storklike, on one leg at a time, and unconcerned, the Maasai herdsman lets time pass."

The Masai tribe is believed to have

*Above: Masai cattlemen
beside a new trough.
Opposite: The Rift Valley.*

originated in North Africa. The people moved south about four hundred years ago to Lake Turkana in northern Kenya. A tribe of skilled warriors, they battled their way farther south into the grasslands of central and southern Kenya and northern Tanzania. Other tribes feared the powerful Masai warriors and fell back into forest areas where Masai fighting tactics were less effective. This left the Masai in control of large open areas of grassy plains where they could tend and protect their large cattle herds.

The Masai had a firm grip on the land until the late 1800s. Then they began to weaken from fighting among themselves and from disease. In 1880, an outbreak of rinderpest cut down the size of their herds. In 1892, the Masai were hit by a smallpox epidemic. Other tribes, including Kikuyu farmers, attacked and began to take away their land and cattle. Then Europeans who came to eastern Africa began to take over much of the Masai land for farming crops, such as coffee and tea.

Since then the government of Kenya has taken away more and more Masai land. Large areas of potential farmland have been sold to whomever wants to buy them. Even larger areas of savanna lands have been turned into national parks and game reserves. The once-powerful warriors now serve mainly to protect their village's cattle from wild animals. While most Kenyans, including other tribes and even other groups of Masai, have turned to farming on better land, the Pastoral Masai cling to cattle-herding on poor savanna grazing lands that nobody else wants.

The Pastoral Masai culture thrived for hundreds of years because its grasslands environment was perfect for grazing. That environment has seen many changes, primarily a change to farming. Because the Pastoral Masai have not changed as well, their culture no longer thrives.

THE TRADITIONAL MASAI SETTLEMENT

The typical settlement of Pastoral Masai has been a village, known as a *kraal*. One or more families may live in a kraal, but it's built as much for cattle as for people. The center area is left open so that the cattle can be driven in and kept safely overnight. A circular outer fence is often built with prickly thorn bushes to keep out wild animals and thieves. The greater the need for protection, the thicker the fence.

The housing in a kraal is small and temporary. Huts are made with tree branches, grass, and cow dung. First, the oblong shape of the house to be built is scratched into the dirt. Then holes are dug around the edge and filled with large branches. Smaller branches are tied together on top of the larger ones and bent to the desired shape. Leafy parts of the branches are woven together to fill in open areas, and grass is packed in all around. Then, to seal the hut against rain and cold, the sides and top are plastered with cow dung.

Most huts are about 4 feet (1 m) high, and the inside has only one room. Beds are made with strong branches and covered with soft animal hides. One bed sleeps up to six people. A smaller, more private bed is made for the mother of the family and her young children. A low hearth in the center is used for cooking,

A kraal

A Masai woman building a shelter
of branches, grass, and cow dung

heating, and lighting the hut. Young animals may be kept in a small pen set off at the side. There are no windows. An opening in the top or side is just big enough to let light in and smoke out, and small enough to keep out most flies that swarm around the cattle. All houses in the kraal have the same basic shape, but some vary in their inner arrangement and outer decorations. These decorations often include symbolic markings.

Most Masai settlements consist of several families. The people join together to better protect their cattle and each other. They also share food and work duties. Each family builds its own house and helps build the kraal fence. Larger kraal communities may have as many as twenty houses. Families who are especially friendly may stay together when the time comes to look for better land. Kraals are built far enough apart to keep the cattle of one from mixing with those of another.

PASTORAL MASAI CUSTOMS AND BELIEFS

The Pastoral Masai have a unique family system that determines who lives where and who does what. Men are divided into three main age groups—youth, warriors, and elders—each with different duties and privileges. Women are generally divided between the married and the unmarried. Only women build the kraal huts. Only men build the kraal fences.

The Masai elders decide where their families will settle, at least until they must move on to find better land. They must continually look for areas that have enough

water and grass and little wind. They look for land that is level, with few rocks so that the cattle can sleep in comfort. They often choose higher places for the village, so that those who stay at home during the day can easily watch over the children and grazing herds.

According to Masai custom, the husband heads the family, and the wife is responsible for running his household. Masai men can marry only when they become elders, but they are allowed to have more than one wife. Each elder has his own entrance to the kraal. When he gets married, his wife builds a house for him on the right side of his entrance. His second wife builds on the left side; his third wife builds on the right next to the first wife, and so on.

The husband spends a great amount of time at the kraal looking after his cattle, property, and family. He must try to meet the needs of each wife and her children for food and protection. If he fails, a wife may go back to live with her parents. The Masai wives cook, sew, clean house, fetch water, gather firewood, and teach their daughters these things to prepare them for marriage. The wives bear as many children as possible, because children are very important to the Masai. With children, the Masai believe, a man's cattle will always be taken care of and his name will live forever. Wives take care of their young children, although everyone in the village looks after all of the children.

Young children are given minor chores, like herding lambs, to prepare them for their duties later in life. But mostly they play games. They especially enjoy making miniature kraals.

The warriors are divided into junior and senior groups. Junior warriors live with their families and share in kraal duties. Senior warriors go off to live in a separate kraal, known as a *manyatta*. When sons are ready to become senior warriors, their mothers build them a circle of shelters covered with animal hides. They always build forty-nine, because the Masai consider that to be their lucky number. Inside that circle, they make a smaller circle of lion-grass mats to be used in the warrior-making ceremonies. The warriors themselves build the surrounding fence for their manyatta.

Warriors live in the manyatta until they become elders and start their own kraals. They are joined by their mothers, young unmarried women they choose to stay with them, and junior elders who instruct them in Masai customs. In each manyatta house, the mother builds a private bed for herself and another for her warrior son and the young woman staying with him. But the warriors and the elders who instruct them own everything in the manyatta. Warriors may visit the homes of their parents, but some people must always stay at the manyatta to protect it.

All young Masai men want to become warriors, because the warriors are admired for their strength and courage. The people trust their warriors to protect the village, and in return, the villagers give them freedom to do what they want. Because the warriors have a special place of honor within the Masai society, their manyattas are closest to the best grazing land and water supply in the area. Warriors usually stay together in groups and share everything they have with each other. In the past Masai warriors fought battles to defend their people and increase their herds. Now their role is more ceremonial—to bring pride, excitement, and a sense of adventure to the villages.

Parents give their warrior sons cattle of their own, and warriors often add to their supply by raiding neighboring herds. Their purpose, besides protecting the village against wild animals and enemies, is to form as big a herd as they can. That is the goal of every Masai male, because the Masai measure a man's worth by the number of cattle he owns. The Masai give each male child a few small animals to raise and, with luck and care, the animals multiply as the child grows up into adulthood. The larger the herd, the richer the owner. A Masai who owns fifty head of cattle is considered fairly well off. Some herds are as large as one thousand cattle. Cattle raiding by Masai warriors was once considered a colorful custom. Now the government of Kenya forbids cattle raiding, although there is no effective way to stop it. Village elders brand their cattle with distinctive markings to discourage raiding.

The Masai have a deep respect for the land. All decisions regarding how it is to be used are made by the Masai elders, who are admired for their wisdom. They are also looked to by the Masai for their guidance and leadership in governing the Masai villages. Together the elders discuss and solve daily problems, make sure Masai laws and customs are kept, give out

Masai warriors

Above: Masai men and women dressed for a ceremony.
Opposite: A Masai warrior in full ceremonial regalia.

all medicine to the sick, and offer advice to younger men on all matters. They also head their own families. Junior elders from many villages often walk long distances to gather with and listen to senior elders, who decide together what is best for the Masai lands and people. Elders are known among the Masai for their love of truth and fine speech. The older they become, the more respect they get. The most respected Masai elder is the *Laibon*, whom the Masai believe is descended from God. And God, the Masai believe, gave them all land and cattle.

Masai elders pass on their respect for the land to their young. They teach their children to honor the cattle, Masai traditions, and their elders. Most Masai are strict with their children, whom they love and value as the future of their tribe. The children receive no formal education. They learn Masai customs and duties by watching their elders, doing what they are told to do, and listening to proverbs, sayings, and stories. Stories are told often, but only at night when the cattle are safe inside the kraal.

Ceremonies are a big part of Masai life. The people wear colorful beads and smear their bodies with *ocher*, a powdered red mineral mixed with fat or water, for ceremonial decoration. The ceremony that initiates young men into warriorhood is probably the most colorful and important of the four major ceremonies Masai men perform as they enter new stages of life. Each includes the ritual killing of an animal to prove bravery, blessings from elders, head shaving, dancing, singing, and feasting. Ceremonies are also held to induct Masai girls into womanhood, but

mostly Masai women help in carrying out the ceremonies for the men.

The Masai travel little other than to move their herds to find pastures and water. Their grasslands have no roads, only wide-open plains. Masai who do travel receive a warm welcome in any kraal. They are always offered a place to stay in the kraal, according to their age group. Because the Masai love their cattle and believe that all cattle rightfully belong to them, they consider any outsider who owns cattle their enemy. Nevertheless, Masai villagers are friendly and courteous to anyone who treats them as equals.

THE IMPORTANCE OF CATTLE

Cattle are the main source of food for the people of Sowakla and other Pastoral Masai villagers. Most Masai do not eat plants of any kind, because they have little water for raising crops, no way to store them, and, most important, a firm belief that plants are inferior to cattle. But the Masai generally do not kill their cows for their meat, because they respect them. And they do not kill wild game for food for the same reason. Only the warriors kill lions as a way to prove their bravery.

The Masai mostly drink cow's milk, either fresh or sour. The women milk the cows twice a day. They collect and store the milk in large gourds called *calabashes*. These are cut from vines, dried and scooped out, and decorated. Then, for cleaning, twigs from wild olive trees are burned in them, the embers are removed, and the insides are scrubbed with long sticks. The olive twigs give the milk a

Young men dancing

smoky flavor that the Masai enjoy, but outsiders find distasteful. Calabashes are also used to store honey beer, a strong drink that Masai adults like.

When milk is less plentiful, especially during the dry season, the Masai drink the blood of a weakened cow. Warriors may drink the blood of a healthy animal to gain strength. In either case, an arrow tip is used to make a cut in the cow's jugular vein, neither killing nor hurting the animal, so that the blood can be drawn out. Sometimes the blood is mixed with milk for drinking.

Most food is shared within the Masai community. Cattle are killed only on important ceremonial occasions or when food is scarce. When they are killed, everyone in the village joins in to eat. Milk and meat are never eaten at the same time, because the Masai believe that the combination gives people tapeworm or causes the cow to be cursed. When the food supply is especially limited, some Masai eat a cereal made by mixing corn-meal with water.

The Masai live by a *subsistence economy*. That is, they use what they own to meet their needs rather than sell goods on the market to make money. They have no money. Their main source of livelihood is their cattle, although they also may keep small flocks of sheep and goats. In some cases, they trade stock or hides for other things they need.

A Masai boy drinking cattle blood

Cattle provide for most Pastoral Masai needs. The Masai use cow urine as medicine. In addition to using cow milk and blood as food, and dung for building kraal huts, the Masai use cattle hides for making bed covers, ropes, shoes, and some clothing, although less clothing than in the past. Now many Masai use factory-made cloth for their colorful outfits.

HOW THE PEOPLE USE THE ENVIRONMENT

The Masai use the environment in many ways. They rely on the savanna's trees, plants, and herbs to cure their ills. The bark of the cassia tree, for example, is used to treat stomach pains. Tree branches are gathered for firewood to cook food and heat Masai huts as well as for supports in building them.

Grass has great practical value to the Masai because their cattle feed on it. They have a saying: "God gave us cattle and grass—without grass there are no cattle, and without cattle there are no Masai." Grass is used by the women to weave mats, called *esos*, that make pens for small animals inside kraal huts.

But grass means more to the Masai as a symbol. During the dry periods, the women tie grass to their clothing and pray for rain. Grass is given by one Masai to another when he wishes to make peace. When a Masai dies, he is laid out on open ground with a clump of grass in his hand.

Masailand cattle number an estimated three million, more cattle per person than in any other Kenya area or tribe.

The Pastoral Masai practice of grazing large herds of cattle in limited areas has made poor environmental conditions worse. In earlier times, when herds multiplied, the Pastoral Masai could move them on to better areas. Now there are few better areas to move to. With the population of Kenya growing, more and more land is being taken over for farming to feed the people. Areas that have enough water and grass for farming either are owned by farmers now or are too crowded with Pastoral Masai and their large herds to support all of them. Other areas that do not have enough water and grass for farming are available to the Pastoral Masai. Their population is growing only slightly, but the number of cattle they graze is increasing steadily.

In some cases, Masai cattle destroy the land. What happens is that the cattle eat all of the grass in a limited area of grazing lands. When it rains, the hard, dry, black-earth soil, left without its grassy cover, cannot hold the water. Dust that had been valuable soil washes away, and most of the rainfall evaporates, or disappears. New growth of savanna grasses is reduced, especially during the longer dry periods, leaving wild animals and large numbers of cattle to starve. During the severe drought of 1960-1961, for example, about a third of a million cattle died. This is happening again in the 1980s, though not to as great an extent as in Ethiopia to the north. When many cattle starve, many Masai starve.

Wild animals move freely over the savanna to graze and drink water in smaller numbers in a variety of places. Their manure is thus spread out over the countryside, fertilizing the soil and helping savanna grasses to grow back again. But Masai cattle are grazed in one spot seven or eight hours a day for several months, often drinking from a watering hole until it dries up. They strip the land of its grasses, and their manure piles up around the watering hole where it does nothing to bring the grasses back.

The Masai are trying to take good care of the land. They often set fire to the grasslands to cut back the growth of unwanted bushes and trees. This allows for better growth of the red oat grasses that their cattle feed on, and it kills many dangerous snakes that easily hide in the grasses. However, what really needs to be done to save the land, the Masai either cannot do or cannot afford to do. They need to move from grazing lands before they are destroyed, but they usually have no other place to go. They need to limit the size of their herds, but if they do, they may go hungry. They need to increase their water supplies, but they do not know how. The government wants them to take up farming and learn proper farming methods, but they do not want to give up cattle-herding.

THE MASAI AND THE FUTURE

Life is very different now for the Masai living just a few miles away from the Sowakla village. The people of the neighboring village of Olosh Oiber built a dam a few years ago with the help of an Amer-

Watching over grazing cattle

Above: A small farm in a typical settlement in Kenya. Opposite: Deep gully erosion has added to the problems of the Masai.

ican missionary. Instead of traveling three miles a day to fetch water as they used to, the Masai women of Olosh Oiber draw it from a large tank a short walk away. Now they have plenty of water for their cattle. While the Sowakla people and other cattle-herding Masai must move out of their villages during the long dry season to look for water, the people of Olosh Oiber can stay by their grazing lands year-round.

As a result, the villagers of Olosh Oiber have given up many Pastoral Masai traditions. They can now build their houses to last a long time. Concrete is laid over a frame of chicken wire, and windows are made of plastic. The houses have raised stoves, chimneys, and plenty of room for the people to live comfortably. The people now eat vegetables from gardens made possible by the dam and fish from the waters behind the dam. The children go to school.

Olosh Oiber may be the Masai village of the future. But most Pastoral Masai do not want help from people outside of the tribe. They are fiercely independent and unwilling to change the way they have lived for hundreds of years. They distrust the Kenyan government. The government has tried to help other tribes obtain water and education for better farming and health care. But little help has been offered to the Masai, because the government wants them to change and they will not do so. While Kenyans move to the future with the growth of farming, most Pastoral Masai prefer to say with cattle-herding.

The Pastoral Masai need good land for their cattle to prosper. Those few individuals who can afford to buy land often don't know how. Some Masai who have lost their land go to Nairobi or other cities to look for work. Because Masai warriors have a reputation for courage in protecting their people, they may be hired as security guards. Other Masai, who have no skills other than cattle-herding, do not find work and end up begging for food in order to survive.

Masai who are near the cities and national parks sometimes sell their finely crafted beadwork, spears, and gourds to tourists. Some get money from tourists in return for posing in native dress for photographers. Many Masai consider this shameful.

The Pastoral Masai do not know how to farm and they do not want to farm. They believe that their God ordered them to be cattle herders. They believe that planting crops destroys the grass that God gave to the Masai for the feeding of their cattle. They believe that planted crops are unholy, but natural grass is good and beautiful.

The relationship that the Pastoral Masai have with their grasslands environment is more than a means of finding food and shelter. It is a relationship based on religious beliefs that influences everything else they do. The many Masai customs and ceremonies, their decorations, songs, and dances all celebrate this relationship and serve to strengthen it. Even the strong love the Masai have for their children rests on their love for their cattle. The Pastoral Masai continue as cattle herders in spite of the threat that farming poses to their future. It would appear that they have no choice. In fact, they choose to raise cattle because that is their God's wish.

4

ABILENE

AN AMERICAN GRASSLANDS VILLAGE

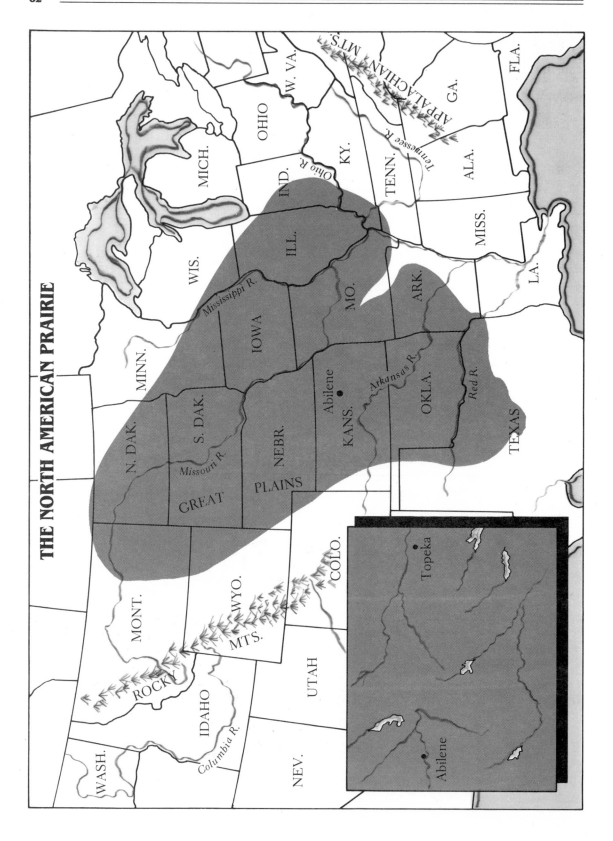

THE NORTH AMERICAN PRAIRIE

Dwight D. Eisenhower grew up in the prairie village of Abilene, Kansas, back in the early 1900s. He felt great pride in his hometown. He believed that the townspeople's influence helped him in later life, first as a leader of American troops in World War II and then as the thirty-fourth president of the United States.

In later visits, President Eisenhower discovered that his hometown was awakening to the sounds of progress. "The nights, once so quiet that the whistle and rumble of a train could be heard rising and falling away across miles of country, are now disturbed by town noises," he noted. Yet, while Abilene grows a little bit bigger, busier, and noisier, it remains a quiet, peaceful prairie village. The people move about at an unhurried pace. The small, plain houses rest on straight, narrow streets that stretch to the town's edge. There tall grain elevators stand in silence with reserves of the prairie's bounty tucked inside. Beyond, grassy farmlands roll gently to the horizon, disturbed only by whispering trees and lazy streams.

VILLAGE, COUNTY, AND AREA

About 8,000 people live in Abilene. The village is the county seat of Dickinson County in central Kansas. Most of the county's 22,000 people live on farmland, the average farm covering 250 acres (101 hectares). Heavily involved in farming and grazing like many other grassland regions, the county is not well populated. The people live far apart on large farms rather than close together in large cities.

Abilene is the biggest of the county's villages. As such, it has become the center of a trade area that extends 55 miles (88 km) north-to-south and 30 miles (48 km) east-to-west. Located at the junction of three railroads—the Union Pacific, the Santa Fe, and the Rock Island—and just as many major highways traveled by freight-carrying truck lines, Abilene is the main shipping point for the area's farm and livestock products. Eight smaller villages extend out from Abilene like spokes in a wheel, because their farm economy centers around Abilene.

THE AMERICAN TALLGRASS PRAIRIE

Abilene lies within North America's tallgrass *prairie*. Many years ago, native tallgrass prairie covered much of the Midwest. A 300-mile-wide (483 km) band stretched about 700 miles (1,126 km) westward from Illinois to Nebraska and Kansas, and it extended northward into Canada and southward into Texas. Fields of very tall grasses, such as Indian grass, bluestem, and switchgrass, stretched for miles in every direction.

Now, most of the tall grasses are gone, having been plowed into farmland. Fields of wild grasses have been replaced with

*Many people of Kansas live
on large, isolated farms.*

The Kansas prairie

fields of wheat. Prairie of shorter grasses survives on the dry Great Plains to the west, but the only remaining large area of native tallgrass prairie can be found in the Flint Hills section of Kansas, not far from Abilene. The Flint Hills's grasses have not been plowed under, only because the soil there is too thin and stony for farming.

Prairie grasses have deep roots and grow to heights ranging from between 3 and 10 feet (1 and 3 m). Trees are scarce, except along stream beds, because the climate and soil conditions favor the growth of grasses. Organic materials from the roots and about 30 inches (76 cm) of precipitation each year combine in developing the rich black-earth soils that produce grain for farmers. Because the area has a fairly long rainy season, and snow accumulates during the winter months and then melts, the soil holds a fairly continuous supply of water. This promotes the healthy growth of grasses.

The temperature averages 55° F (13° C) each year, ranging between 29° F (1.7° C) for January and 78° F (26° C) for July. These are moderate temperatures, partly because the area's latitude and elevation are moderate. Abilene sits at a middle latitude of 39 degrees north and a medium elevation of 1,448 feet (441 m).

The way people live in Abilene is determined to a large extent by the prairie around them. Life there centers on the farming and grazing economy for which the prairie is so well suited. The vast expanse of the prairie, with Abilene located far from the crowds and commotion of the cities, leaves plenty of room for the quiet, small-town lifestyle that has developed there.

THE HISTORY OF ABILENE

Abilene owes its importance in the area to events that took place more than one hundred years ago. Things were not so quiet then.

Timothy Hersey founded Abilene in the late 1850s as a tiny log cabin village and stagecoach stop for passengers heading west. In the years between 1867 and 1872, stockyards full of cattle and hotels full of people took over the village. Abilene's population jumped from 300 to 3,000. Mrs. Hersey chose the name Abilene, meaning "city of the plains," from the Bible. But Abilene soon became a city of cowboys and outlaws, and the Bible got pushed aside in favor of saloons, gambling houses, and gunfights.

This all happened because the railroad came to town. The Kansas-Pacific (later Union Pacific) extended its tracks westward to Abilene in 1867, making the village the perfect place for Texas ranchers to bring their cattle for transport. Cowhands drove the cattle north along the now-famous Chisholm Trail to Abilene. There they were loaded onto railroad cars to be shipped to markets in the East. Over the next five years, Abilene became the loudest, wildest town in the country.

For a while, the gun was the town's only law. Then Abilene hired Tom Smith, a New York City policeman, as its first marshal. Smith's courage won the respect of townspeople and outlaws, but one outlaw shot him a year later. The legendary Wild Bill Hickok became marshal next. He tried to keep Abilene quiet and orderly by shooting anyone who challenged him.

*The first railroad depot
in Abilene*

Loading cattle at Abilene in the 1870s

A corn carnival in Abilene in 1899

He too was murdered before long in a saloon in South Dakota.

WHEAT COMES, THE RAILROADS GO

Abilene would be forever famous for its cowboys and town marshals, but two other things happened that would have a greater impact on the village's future.

One, Abilene became the birthplace of winter wheat. As Wild Bill Hickok was dueling outlaws, the mayor of Abilene was secretly experimenting in wheat production. His success in 1871 at growing winter wheat in fields outside of Abilene helped to turn the Kansas prairie into the nation's breadbasket. Abilene went on to become the center of a prosperous farming region.

Two, the railroad extended its tracks even farther west. In just a few years' time, when the railroad had brought the cattle business to Abilene, the village had gone from quiet and peaceful to wild and lawless. Just as suddenly, when the railroad took the cattle business to other Kansas villages, like Dodge City, Abilene became quiet and peaceful again.

Instead of growing into a large city, Abilene remained a small village. Early leaders laid out Abilene to become a city of 50,000 people. But then they decided to discourage rapid growth, figuring that a small, quiet hometown was better for the people of Abilene than a large, bustling city.

Open land extended in every direction from Abilene's center in those early days. Even so, the streets were set close together, and housing lots were just as small as those in the crowded cities of the East. Setting houses close together allowed the planners room for growth, gave houses some protection from the prairie wind, saved valuable land for farming, and created a sense of community. If people wanted to be an integral part of the community, they lived close to their neighbors in the center of town. If they preferred to be more isolated, they moved out into the more rural surrounding area.

Over the years Abilene grew slowly. President Eisenhower's family, like most families in Abilene at the turn of the century, was devoutly religious. Young Ike's parents, who were strict but loving, often gathered him and his five brothers together for readings from the Bible. Raising the large family on a small income, they taught their children self-sufficiency and sharing. While Ike was going to school and playing football and baseball, he was also responsible for doing a variety of household chores. He earned extra money for his family working at odd jobs.

ABILENE TODAY

Things haven't changed much in Abilene since then. Close family ties are still a big part of the lifestyle. Many of the local businesses are small and family owned. Even the children help to run them. As families move in to Abilene, few move out. Most of the people live their entire lives in Abilene, and many families have three generations living in town. Because the young townspeople often marry each other, many in the village are related to each other. Everyone knows everyone else. The people try to care for each other and raise their children to do the same.

The tracks of the Union Pacific Railroad run east-west through the middle of Abilene, dividing the village into two distinct parts. To the north lie the business district and main streets. Many of Abilene's stores and bigger homes are found here. Modern housing developments have sprung up in a few small pockets, but most of the house were built a long time ago, around or before the turn of the century. Many feature the elegance and ornate design of Victorian architecture.

Most houses in Abilene are made of wood. When they were built many years ago, building materials were not brought in from outside of the area. The people used what was available. Though not plentiful, trees are found on the prairie around Abilene. They supplied the wood for Abilene's houses.

A number of large mansions built by rich cattle owners at that time are still standing. Many have become rundown, because few townspeople have enough money to buy and repair them. Others have been restored and maintained as historical landmarks.

To the south of the railroad, the houses are generally smaller and plainer than those on the north side. This area also includes several tourist attractions, such as "Old Abilene Town" and the buildings that make up the Eisenhower Center.

These tourist attractions bring in large numbers of visitors to Abilene, and its well-developed road system makes the village easy to reach. Interstate highways connect Abilene with the cities of Topeka, the state capital; Kansas City; Wichita;

Denver, Colorado; and Lincoln, Nebraska. All-weather secondary roads connect Abilene with every other village in the trade area. In addition to railroad, truck, and bus service, Abilene has its own airport. It can accommodate twin-motor aircraft and is served by a feeder passenger airline.

CUSTOMS AND BELIEFS

Religion plays a big part in the way Abilene people live. The town has twenty-three churches. Said one minister, "Abilene is the only town I know that has more churches than gas stations." Almost everyone belongs to a church. The village founders passed on their solid religious values to younger generations, who passed them on to their sons and daughters. They created a small-town lifestyle of neighborliness and caring, one that could thrive in the peace and quiet of the prairie, away from the crowds of the big cities.

The people of Abilene do not like too much change of any kind. They like most things the way they are and have been. Things have changed in Abilene over the years—new houses have been built, new businesses have moved in, more young people are leaving to look for better work opportunities—but maybe not quite as quickly or as much as in other places. The people would welcome new industries that would bring more jobs to the area, but *small* industries. A large corporation like General Motors would bring in too many people and change Abilene too much too fast. The people of Abilene would prefer to keep their slow, easy-going, everyone-knows-everyone-else lifestyle.

The citizens of Abilene place great

value on being with and helping each other. Many individuals are active in civic and charitable organizations. The numerous women's clubs and church groups sponsor special events for the community and free-food programs for the needy. Hunter-safety programs and a variety of "how-to" classes are especially popular. The Chamber of Commerce is active in promoting cultural activities as well as business growth.

Abilene's farms produce grain and livestock to feed the nation, but the people also eat what they grow. They enjoy large breakfasts of pancakes and meat and eggs. Suppers of meat and potatoes are common. Much of the food is homegrown and homemade. Many people bake their own bread. For those who do not know how, a "bread fair" is held each year to show them.

Fish and game are plentiful in the area's streams and rolling hills. Because pheasant is especially popular, classes are offered on how to cook it.

THE ECONOMY OF THE REGION

Many of the people of Abilene earn their living from the prairie. Wheat farming is the biggest local industry. A variety of other grain crops are grown as well, including corn, oats, sorghum, and popcorn, which is an Indian variety of corn. The region west of Abilene is known for growing smaller amounts of watermelons, cantaloupes, and potatoes.

Like farmers throughout the Midwest, those in Abilene are facing financial problems. Income decreased for many

Midwestern farmers during the 1970s when the price they got for their products decreased and a long dry period cut down on the size of their harvests. Farmers borrowed money from banks to pay for land and equipment, but in some cases they didn't make enough money from their produce to pay back the loans. Now, while the price farmers get for their products stays low, the value of their land goes down. They need to borrow more money from banks to meet their needs, and the interest rate—the price they must pay banks to borrow—stays high. Many farmers are being forced to sell their farms, or give them up to the banks, because they do not have enough income to keep them going.

The federal government has tried to help farmers. One way has been to offer loans at low interest rates directly to farmers or to banks so that they can offer them to farmers. Another way has been to set prices. The government decides how much money all farmers should get for their products, rather than let buyers and farmers decide, to make sure that farmers get a "fair" price.

The government helps Abilene farmers in still another way. Because often more wheat is grown than is needed—creating a *surplus*—the government pays farmers for *not* growing wheat. The farmers, who naturally want to grow as much as they can and get the highest possible price for it, do not like the idea of getting a lower price for growing less. Because they rely on their own hard work to earn a living, many do not like the idea of taking money from the government, however much it might be. But they have no choice.

Wheat farming is the biggest local industry in Abilene.

A small oil well in the middle of a freshly plowed cornfield. Grain and energy are major state exports.

Farmers around the country are divided in their opinions. Some think that the government can best help farmers solve their problems by controlling production and price levels. Others think that control should be left to the farmers and those who buy from them.

Farmers around Abilene fear that the federal government and banks are slowly taking over their lives. Farmers have a tradition of self-sufficiency. They have always worked for themselves, provided for and taken care of their families, made all of their own decisions, and done things their own way. For the last twenty-five years, as farm prices have failed to rise making money at grain farming has become more difficult. As banks and the government gain more control over the farmers' money supply, they are having more to say about how things are to be done. As farmers gradually lose their independence, they see the way they have always done business undergoing unwanted changes.

Farming replaced cattle as Abilene's main source of income more than a century ago. Now the reverse is beginning to happen. The importance of livestock has been increasing over the last twenty years. The area around Abilene is fast becoming a top producer of livestock, beef cattle and sheep, but also hogs. While government regulation has kept wheat prices at a steady level, some farmers have found bigger profits in rising livestock prices.

OTHER ABILENE BUSINESSES

Businesses related to agriculture are another big part of the local economy. One

business is the processing of farm products. Abilene has several operations that turn grains into livestock feed, such as bulk alfalfa meal and pellets. Another major business is the transporting of farm products by truck and railroad.

Farming and its related occupations are important to Abilene's prosperity. Yet only one-tenth of the area's work force can be counted in this category. Manufacturing, trade, services, and government each employ more area people than does farming. Products made in Abilene include athletic clothing for high school students, western clothing, blasting equipment, and axles. One larger business, Duckwall-Alco Stores, started as a small store in Abilene in 1901. Now, in addition to its general offices and warehousing operations in Abilene, the Duckwall-Alco chain has 167 stores in 14 states. Other major employers include Abilene's Memorial Hospital, the Kansas Power & Light Company, the school system, and the village and county governments.

Abilene claims to be the tourist center of Kansas. Thousands of people come to Abilene each year to see "Old Abilene Town" and the village's many museums and special events. "Old Abilene Town" serves as a memorial to the spirit of the village's sturdy pioneer citizens and as an attraction for tourists who are familiar with Abilene's colorful past. Buildings like the old jailhouse and Alamo Saloon also stand as reminders that Abilene has changed since those early times. The Central Kansas Free Fair, featuring the Wild Bill Hickok Rodeo, a livestock sale, and a tractor-pull contest, attracts especially large crowds. Tourist attractions employ

Drifts of dust cover a farmstead.

Abilene's people and bring money to the local economy.

Having so many different kinds of employers helps to keep Abilene's economy strong. If wheat farming or livestock were the only source of income, and the farms had a poor harvest one year, everyone in the area would be hurt badly by it. But in the balanced economy of Abilene, with many different industries producing income, a poor harvest would not affect as many people as severely. A bad year for farming, for example, might be offset by a good year for tourism. This diversification of economy is especially important to the people of Abilene during a time when farmers throughout the Midwest are losing their farms.

THREATS TO
THE GRASSLANDS
ENVIRONMENT

The farmers around Abilene do not have many poor harvests. Things were different on the prairie fifty years ago, however, when it became the "Dust Bowl." Much of Kansas and the surrounding states suffered several years of scant rainfall during the 1930s. This extended period of drought left the soil powdery and dry. After many years of too much grazing by livestock, too much plowing and planting of wheat fields, and too much cutting of trees, the dry soil had no protection against harsh prairie winds. Wind storms blew large, blinding clouds of dust across the prairie. People often couldn't eat or drink without feeling dust between their teeth. Much of the land's rich topsoil blew away, making it difficult to farm with any success.

Many farmers had no choice but to leave their damaged land. They packed up their belongings and their families and moved away. Some looked for jobs in the cities, where few were to be found. Others looked for new farmland to work in areas that had not turned to dust.

CONSERVATION
IN THE GRASSLANDS

Still other farmers stayed behind and tried new farming methods to restore their farms. Helped by state and federal agencies, and by eight straight years of plentiful rainfall during the 1940s, many succeeded.

Since then, the use of conservation measures has done a great deal to restore the prairie. Planting of trees has helped to hold the soil and water in place by slowing down the prairie winds. Fires are often set to remove dead or undesirable plants and allow for thicker growth of healthy grasses. Abilene has built a modern sewage treatment plant to control pollution and recently completed a project designed to control flooding.

The farmers cannot control the problems that nature brings. One year their fields might be hit with hailstorms; another year they might not get enough rainfall. Long periods of cold weather might shorten the growing season. A tornado might strike.

Farmers have solved many problems by paying more attention to soil fertilization and other proper farming methods. They use *crop rotation*—planting certain crops in sequence with others —to return nutrients to the soil. They use *strip cropping*—planting crops in narrow

bands between bands of grasses—and *contour farming*—planting crops in curving rows along the sides of hills—to prevent erosion and enrich the soil. Along with the use of modern mechanized equipment and improved irrigation systems for supplying water, these methods have produced big increases in farm productivity.

THE FUTURE OF THE KANSAS GRASSLANDS

Before the "Dust Bowl" years, the people of the prairie thought of soil, grass, and water as limitless. They thought of the prairie as something that would be there forever. Now they know differently. Besides favoring conservation methods, most Kansans want to make sure that the Flint Hills tallgrass prairie is preserved. But they have different ideas on how to go about it.

Ranchers own much of the Flint Hills land and use it for grazing their cattle. Preservationists want the government to buy the land from them and turn it into a national park. The ranchers argue that grazing preserves the Flint Hills prairie. What happens to the Flint Hills will not directly affect the people of Abilene or their economy, but the decision will be important to them. They too are divided over how the tallgrass prairie should be cared for, but they have one thing in common: They want the prairie preserved, because they love and respect the land they live on.

The farmers of Kansas are concerned with soil conservation.

5

A COMPARISON OF THREE GRASSLANDS REGIONS

Viriatino in the forest-steppe region of the Soviet Union, the Masai village of Sowakla on the African savanna in Kenya, and Abilene, Kansas, on the North American prairie are similar and different. They are similar in many ways because they have one common element, a grasslands location. They are unalike for two reasons: the elements that make up each grasslands region are different, and the people who live there have responded to these elements in different ways.

THE PHYSICAL ELEMENTS

The main physical elements that make up each grasslands region are soil, plant cover, precipitation, and temperature. All three regions have black-earth soil. The plant cover in each is distinct, and is used in different ways, mainly because of differences in temperature and precipitation.

Major factors in determining temperature are latitude and elevation. In general, the farther away from the equator and the higher the elevation, the lower the temperature. Sowakla is at a relatively high elevation, but at a latitude of only about 1° south of the equator. Therefore, the savanna has hot tropical air. The Abilene prairie, at a middle latitude of 39° north and a medium elevation, has moderate temperatures. Viriatino lies on lowlands, but the latitude, further north at 53°, produces the generally cooler air of the forest-steppe region.

Precipitation has a bigger influence on plant cover in the grasslands. The three regions described in this book get about the same amount of rain, but they differ in when the rain falls. In areas like the African savanna, most of the precipitation comes during only half the year. The growth of trees and some grasses is limited, because there is not enough water during the long dry season. When precipitation does occur, few trees and grasses are there to hold the moisture. Much of the precipitation evaporates under the hot sun, thus continuing the cycle of reduced moisture that limits plant growth. The American prairie and the Soviet forest-steppe region have a longer rainy season, and snow accumulates during the winter. This gives the grasses a more continuous water supply for better growth. More trees can grow, especially in the cooler air of the forest-steppe, and the trees help to protect the grasses against evaporation and strong winds.

All of these elements work together in an ongoing process. Changes in rainfall and temperature are constantly making changes in the soil and its plant cover, and changes in the soil and its plant cover effect each other.

The various combinations of elements are the same within each grasslands region. Because latitude has a major influence on the climate, the zones of roughly similar plant cover run generally in an east-to-west direction. In many cases, other environmental zones with different characteristics run parallel to them. A good example is the Soviet Union, where narrow east-west bands of mixed and broad-leaf forest to the north and bands of steppe, semi-desert, and desert to the south are parallel with the forest-steppe.

PEOPLE AND NATURE SHAPE THE ENVIRONMENT

Human differences have combined with natural differences in determining how the three grasslands regions have developed. The natural growth of large areas of grasses in each region made them ideal for grain farming and cattle grazing. In the Masai grasslands, where the extreme heat and dry air limit the possibilities for farming, the Pastoral Masai were able to gain control of the land for cattle herding. The soil and climate of the forest-steppe gave the farming people of Viriatino rich land and trees that protected it against invasions from the south. Only conflicts among the people over control of the land kept them from making it as productive for farming and grazing as it could be. The pioneer settlers of Abilene found fertile prairie lands free for the taking. After getting sidetracked by cattle shipping, for which outsiders chose Abilene because of its location rather than its grasslands, the people gradually developed the land for both farming and livestock raising.

Viriatino, Abilene, and Masai villagers all started with the idea that the grasslands would live forever. They believed they would have an endless supply of rich soil and clean water to use as they wished. The people of Abilene learned from the terrible experience of the Dust Bowl years that careful farming and conservation methods are needed to keep the prairie alive and well. After years of poor farming methods and no conservation efforts, central government planners of the Soviet Union decided that collective farming with improved methods and machinery would restore the land and make it more productive. The Masai recognize now that supplies of water and grass for their cattle are limited. Their best recourse would be to take up farming. But even if their traditional beliefs allowed them to practice farming, they would have to learn how to farm the land in a way that would keep it rich and productive.

HOW DISTANCE AFFECTS CHANGE

The people of these villages want to stay close to the land that has always supported them and close to each other. They see influences from outside their villages as threats to their independence and way of life. They have been able to resist change because their villages are small and far from the cities. While the development of industry has attracted larger numbers of people to work in the cities and other regions, grain farming and cattle grazing require fewer people in larger areas of open land. Villages that depend on farming or grazing for their livelihood are scattered across the grasslands, far from the reach of people who would change them. Still, Abilene and Viriatino are not immune to outside influences such as newspapers, television, and radio. And Sowakla is not totally removed from change either. In all three areas, it is the older people who resist change the most. Most younger people are more willing to seek new opportunities and new ways.

GOVERNMENTS AND CULTURE

The governments of the Soviet Union and Kenya want the grassland peoples to change. They want the people to alter their approach to the land and their culture. The Soviet Union started collective farming as a way to make farming more efficient and productive. But the Soviet government also started a cultural revolution to bring "backward" villages like Viriatino more in line with the modern ways of the cities. Government efforts to educate the village people to dress, act, and think more like city people have narrowed somewhat the culture gaps between them. The government feels that eliminating the basic differences between the village and the city will result in more rapid growth and a better life for the village people.

The Kenyan government, and most Kenyans, view farming and industry as the keys to the country's future. They want the Pastoral Masai to give up cattle-herding and, along with that, their traditional ways. However, although the government of Kenya encourages the Masai to develop water supplies, build health centers, and educate themselves, it offers little help in showing them how to accomplish those things.

The United States government has no desire to change the people of Abilene. But government policies, such as the regulation of grain prices, have brought about changes in the Abilene economy and, to some extent, in how the people live.

NEW OPPORTUNITIES

As grasslands populations continue to grow, more demands are being made on the land. In the past there was plenty of land for everyone. This is no longer so. Almost all suitable land on the Kansas prairie and in the forest-steppe surrounding Viriatino has been turned into farms. Much of the Masai grazing land has been taken over for farming.

Grasslands people still have opportunities, but they are different opportunities. Even though American farmers face serious financial problems, grain farming is still the biggest part of Abilene's economy. But with a balanced economy that includes livestock grazing, tourism, and a variety of small industries, the people of Abilene face a brighter future than people in other prairie villages who rely entirely on grain farming for their income. Collective farmers of Viriatino must rely on the success of the collective system in making and keeping the land productive. In some instances, the collective farming system has been highly successful. In other instances, it has failed. But the people of Viriatino are finding more and more opportunities in the industries that are developing in nearby towns and cities. Finally, the Pastoral Masai have the chance to give up cattle-herding for farming, but the opportunity is limited. They own little land that is suitable for farming; they do not know how to farm; and they do not believe in farming. Unless they change in these three ways, as they are being asked to do, their opportunities are likely to become more and more limited.

The grasslands environment is more than grass and soil. It is also people. What you see in grasslands villages is the product of people and the physical elements around them changing with each other.

GLOSSARY

Acacia-Thermeda—a zone of open grasslands extending about 200 miles (322 km) east-to-west on the southern side of Kenya's Mau Hills.

Brigades—groups of about one hundred farm workers each, permanently assigned to one kind of work on a kolkholz.

Calabash—large gourds in which Masai women store milk and other beverages.

Chernozem—black-earth soils, among the most fertile in the world.

Contour farming—planting crops in curving rows along the side of hills in order to prevent erosion and enrich the soil.

Core areas—areas in a region where many objective and subjective elements of culture and environment overlap.

Cossacks—adventurous soldiers who helped the Russians defeat the Tatars.

Crop rotation—planting certain crops in sequence with others in order to return nutrients to the soil.

Culture—a way of life devised by people for getting along with the environment and each other.

Engai—the god of the Masai.

Environment—the physical features of the world around us: air, water, plant life, soil, and rocks.

Esos—grass mats used by the Masai to make pens for small animals inside kraal huts.

Forest-steppe—a narrow band of grasslands and trees that runs across the European part of the Soviet Union.

Grasslands—land on which the dominant plant form is grass.

Intelligentsia—the better educated, very influential citizens of the Soviet Union.

Keekonyokie—one of the smaller of Masailand's twelve sections.

Kolkhoz—a large collective farm found in the Soviet Union, formed by the Soviet government's taking control of many small farms and joining them together.

Kraal—a Masai village.

Kulaks—wealthy Russian peasants of the nineteenth and early twentieth centuries.

Kvass—a Russian fermented beverage made from dried black bread; sometimes prepared with vegetables.

Laibon—the most respected Masai elder.

Mahorka—a variety of tobacco grown in the Soviet Union.

Manyatta—a kraal in which Masai senior warriors live.

Model—a simplification of the real thing; for example, the model of a region.

Moran—a warrior of the Masai tribes.

Oblast—a small political division of the Soviet Union.

Ocher—a powdered red mineral mixed with fat or water; used by the Masai for ceremonial decoration.

Prairie—a large area of level or rolling land, the American grasslands.

Reforestation—planting of young trees or seeds to replace trees that were cut down.

Region—an area within which elements of culture or environment are similar.

Savanna—tropical or subtropical grasslands.

Shelterbelts—barriers of trees and shrubs that protect crops from the wind and storms.

Soviet—an elected governing council in the Soviet Union or a Communist country.

Strip cropping—planting crops in narrow bands between bands of grasses in order to prevent erosion and enrich the soil.

Subsistence economy—a system in which people such as the Masai use what they own to meet their needs rather than sell goods on the market to make money.

Surplus—the result when farmers grow more of a certain crop than is needed.

Tropical continental—a hot, dry climate such as that found in Masailand, also called *tropical savanna*.

Tropical savanna—see *Tropical continental*.

Tsar—the name for the Russian ruler before the Communist Revolution of 1917.

FOR
FURTHER
READING

Binyon, Michael. *Life in Russia*. New York: Pantheon Books, 1983.

Brown, Leslie. *The Life of the African Plains*. New York: McGraw-Hill Book Company, 1972.

Farney, Dennis. "The Tallgrass Prairie: Can It Be Saved?" *National Geographic*, Vol. 157, No. 1 (January 1980), pp. 37-61.

Horton, Catherine. *Grasslands and People*. Morristown, N.J.: Silver Burdett, 1982.

Lydolph, Paul. *Geography of the U.S.S.R.*, 3rd. ed. New York: John Wiley & Sons, 1977.

Madson, John. *Where the Sky Began— Land of the Tallgrass Prairie*. Boston: Houghton Mifflin Company, 1982.

Naden, Corinne. *Grasslands Around the World*. New York: Franklin Watts, 1970.

Saitoti, Tepelit Ole. *Maasai*. New York: Harry N. Abrams, 1980.

INDEX